AMISH PATTERNS
FOR MACHINE QUILTING

PAT HOLLY AND SUE NICKELS

DOVER PUBLICATIONS, INC.
Mineola, New York

This book is dedicated to our families; Jack, Emmy, and Alyssa
Mozdzen and Tim, Jessi, and Ashley Nickels! We couldn't do what
we love to do without your love and support

Published in Canada by General Publishing Company, Ltd.,
30 Lesmill Road, Don Mills, Toronto, Ontario.

Bibliographical Note

Amish Patterns for Machine Quilting is a new work, first published by Dover Publications, Inc., in 1997.

Library of Congress Cataloging-in-Publication Data

Holly, Pat.
    Amish patterns for machine quilting / Pat Holly and Sue
Nickels.
        p.   cm.
    Includes bibliographical references.
    ISBN 0-486-29876-0 (pbk.)
    1. Machine quilting—Patterns. 2. Quilts, Amish. I.
Nickels, Sue. II. Title.
TT835.H55622   1997
746.46'041—dc21   97-29904
                                                       CIP

Manufactured in the United States of America
Dover Publications, Inc., 31 East 2nd Street , Mineola, N.Y. 11501

INTRODUCTION

When choosing quilting designs, we often look at old quilts for inspiration. Among the best resources for beautiful quilting designs are antique Amish quilts. This book gives you a wide variety of designs inspired by these striking and timeless quilts. Included are instructions for how to quilt the designs using your sewing machine, but you may quilt by hand if you desire. We want you to consider these designs as a starting point. Feel free to change the size, shape, or any other aspect to make the design fit your quilt. The designs will look lovely on your own Amish-style quilt or any other style quilt you choose to make. Some will also work as appliqué designs. Please make these designs your own and use them however you want.

We found that studying the Amish people helped us to understand why they made quilts the way they did. We want to show how you can use their ideas in the world of modern machine quilting. We believe it is possible to make a beautiful quilt with "fine" stitching entirely by machine. The quilts shown on the covers of this book are good examples of Amish-style quilts using patterns from this book.

These designs can add an element of history and a bit of the beauty left to us by some of the most creative and masterful quilters in our past.

History

Like many immigrants, the Amish came to America so that they could worship in their chosen manner. The Amish are a conservative offshoot of the Mennonites, a group of Christian Anabaptists that were started in the sixteenth century. In the late 1600s, Jakob Ammann, believing that the group was not strict enough, split from the Mennonites. By the 1700's, both the Mennonites and Amish in Europe saw the opportunity for religious freedom in the New World and came to America. The first Amish settled in Pennsylvania early in the eighteenth century. More immigrated between 1815 and 1860.

Few Amish quilts dating earlier than 1860 have been found. Never completely isolated, the Amish have always traded with the "English" (anyone not Amish), allowing for a certain amount of outside influence on Amish culture. By 1860, the Amish population in America was large enough and well enough established to resist these influences. The Amish refusal to participate in any fighting during the Civil War helped insure and maintain their separation from the "English." The availability of cheap, factory-made fabrics at this time encouraged a surge of quiltmaking. The insulation of the Amish community from outside influences resulted in a radically different style of quilting.

The Amish strive to live a plain and simple life. Most live by farming and use horses and mules for transportation and to work the fields. Congregations are deliberately kept small (around 30 families), so that worship services can be held in homes. The Amish feel there should be no visual symbols of luxury in their communities. The home should contain only those items that are necessary. Shades on the windows are allowed, but not curtains. A calendar, family record, or clock may be the only items hung on the wall. Hooked rugs on the floor are acceptable, but upholstered chairs or sofas are not. Because they are useful objects, many rugs and quilts were made. It is acceptable, in fact, required, that these objects be made with skill and beauty.

The Amish believe pride and willfulness cause disharmony. To the Amish, pride is the cardinal sin. They value humility and try to achieve happiness through helping their family and friends. By following a lifestyle unlike that of the outside world, they are able to focus on those parts of life that contribute to their faith and family. They do not believe modern inventions are inherently evil, but avoid them to help keep their community from being overly concerned with material comfort and success. Before making any changes, the Amish leaders try to determine what effect the change will have on the community. Rules cover what tools and machines are used, how people are to behave, and even what colors are acceptable to wear. The same fabrics used to make clothing are used to make quilts.

Understanding how the Amish lived (and continue to live) helps us understand how their quilts came about. Certain colors were allowed. Certain designs were passed down, becoming a family tradition. Because there was so little influence from outside, quiltmakers had no rules about what colors went with other colors. This led to the early, simple, color-field quilts displaying very dramatic and surprising color combinations.

As the communities grew, some Amish desired change. They broke off from their original communities and moved from Pennsylvania to Ohio and northern Indiana. When these Midwestern groups made quilts, they were influenced by the less conservative attitudes held by their members.

The Lancaster Amish quilts have certain characteristics in common and are quite unlike what most American quiltmakers were making at the time. The quilts were usually square, made with large, geometric shapes, often with a central medallion design (Diamond in the Square, Bars, and Sunshine and Shadow are some examples). Elaborate quilting on the large borders and in the center areas was usually done with contrasting thread. Black fabric was seldom used and there was no depictive imagery (appliqué was rare). Solid-colored, fine wool fabrics in deep and dark colors such as magenta, burgundy, mauve, navy, peacock blue, green, a rich brown, and shades of gray were often used.

The Midwestern Amish (Ohio and Indiana) in general made rectangular quilts. Often these were made in repeat block units (baskets, baby's blocks, stars), like the more traditional American quilts of the same time. Borders were smaller and less elaborately quilted. Fabrics were still solid colors, no calicoes or prints. Lighter colors were allowed, including yellow and pink. White was not used until later; the Amish reserved this color for funerals. Black was used with the lighter colors. Cotton fabric was used often. Quilters were allowed to participate in relief projects, making quilts for others, something prohibited in Pennsylvania.

The historical (1860–1930) Amish quilts of Pennsylvania and the Midwest provide us with a wealth of inspiration. We have studied many of these quilts and made our own interpretation of the quilting designs. Our goal was to create Amish-style quilting designs that could be stitched on the sewing machine (or by hand if you like). We have tried to maintain the integrity of the designs while adapting them for ease of stitching with the machine. We have used them on our own Amish-style quilts and hope you will be inspired to use them on your quilts.

GENERAL INSTRUCTIONS

Supplies Used

Sewing Machine
A sewing machine is the essential supply for machine quilting. Any sewing machine can do quilting, although some machines can only do straight lines. Remember to keep your sewing machine in good working condition and to clean and oil it regularly.

Walking or Even-Feed Foot
A walking foot is used to quilt straight lines. The walking foot acts like a top set of feed dogs, feeding all the layers of the quilt through the machine evenly.

Darning Foot
A darning foot is essential for free-motion quilting. The feed dogs must be lowered or covered, depending on your sewing machine. This technique enables you to do all of the curved quilting designs in this book.

Thread
We have used cotton threads for the quilts seen on the covers of this book. We recommend 100% cotton threads for the look achieved here. For the top of the quilt, we have used a few different weight threads. A 50-weight thread is the average weight for machine quilting. A 30-weight thread is heavier and will show more on your quilt. We have used both of these thread weights on our quilts. You will have more success with the better quality 100% cotton threads versus the less expensive cotton/polyester blends. For the bobbin, we use 50-weight 100% cotton in a color that is complementary to the threads used on the top of the quilt. When choosing a thread color, remember that if the thread is close in color to the fabric you are quilting on, your stitches will be less noticeable. If you are very comfortable with free-motion quilting, choose a color that contrasts and shows off your stitching. If you are very new to machine quilting, a good choice is transparent nylon thread. We like to use .004-weight transparent nylon thread for our machine quilting. We used this almost exclusively when we first started machine quilting and were very happy with the results. Now that we

are more comfortable with machine quilting, we want to show off our stitching and like using a variety of threads.

Sewing Machine Needles
80/12 is the preferred size needle for machine quilting with 50-weight cotton threads. A 75/11 machine quilting needle works well with transparent nylon thread. Heavier threads may need a larger-eyed needle such as a 90/14.

Safety Pins
We like to use size 0 or 1 brass safety pins to baste our quilts. Pin basting works better than thread basting for machine quilting because of the small stitches used. It would be difficult to remove the basting threads.

Batting
There are many different types of batting available for machine quilting. In keeping with the traditional look of the Amish quilts, we used cotton batting. We have also found that cotton battings are easier to machine-quilt than polyester battings. Follow the manufacturer's' instructions for how far apart to quilt with a particular batting.

Markers
There are many types of marking tools available today. A Berol Veri-thin marking pencil is a good choice for most fabrics. Silver works for most fabrics; white works well on dark colors. If you do not mark too hard the lines come off easily. We also use a wash-out marker for light fabrics (being sure to test before using and following the manufacturer's instructions). Another choice for dark fabrics is a white chalk pencil. This comes out very easily—sometimes too easily with marks disappearing before the quilt is done.

Rubber Glove "Fingers"
When doing free-motion quilting, control of the quilt is very important. Sue likes to use fingertips (knuckle length) cut from rubber kitchen gloves to help grip the fabric. Finger "cots," finger wraps, and secretary fingers are also available for this purpose.

How to Use the Patterns in This Book

Choosing Patterns For Your Quilt

Look at the patterns in the book and choose the designs that you like and would look nice with the style of your quilt. It helps to look at other quilts and see what attracted you to them. These patterns are inspired by Amish-style quilts, but will look nice on many different styles of quilts. If the designs you have chosen do not fit on your quilt, you can use a copy machine to enlarge or reduce the designs to fit. Feel free to adapt or change any of these patterns to work for your particular quilt.

Most of the patterns in this book have short instructions for quilting included with them. Where needed, you will find arrow directions for your free-motion quilting. A small diamond (◆) will indicate where to start sewing. To quilt the feathers, use the feather sewing directions on Plate 30. Before you stitch, be sure that you understand the order of quilting, so that you can make the sewing as continuous as possible. Practice by using your finger to trace over the small design with the arrows. Sometimes you will retrace a line (like "vein" lines inside a leaf) so that you can get back out to a main line. Try to stitch on top of or as close as possible to the line already stitched.

Some of the patterns in the book are more loosely interpreted. We will explain these in this next section.

Designs for Large Areas—Triangles and Borders

We saw many Amish quilts with floral sprays and floral wreaths. These are too large to include in this book, but we have given you all the components you need to draw your own. These will be custom made to fit your quilt.

The floral sprays are seen in large corner triangle areas. Look at the small drawing in the corner of Plate 26. Use a piece of paper the same size as the area on your quilt. Start with a main center stem and place a rose (or any other flower) on the end. Draw stems coming off the main stem and place tulips on the end of these stems. Add more stems and leaves to fill the area. It is very common to see the use of double lines for the stems. Sometimes every element—stems, flowers, and leaves—were all quilted with two lines stitched close together. Remember this as you are designing the quilting for your quilt. It is not hard to add that second line of quilting.

Floral wreaths (Plate 27) are frequently seen on large borders. If you want the wreaths to repeat evenly to fit a certain area, try making a small sketch to scale on graph paper. That way you will see how large the oval of the wreath needs to be. The flower that is in the center and connects adjoining wreaths is often placed so that the wreath lines touch just the outside of the flower. There is usually a flower on the top and bottom of the oval. Leaves can come off singly or in groups of three connected by a stem. They can also point to the outside and inside of the oval.

We also saw a large vine filling in an outer border with flowers and leaves similar to those in the sprays and wreaths. Start with paper the width of your border. Draw a big "U" across the width, leaving about one inch at the top and bottom. Trace this shape onto another piece of paper. Turn it upside down and put it under your border next to your first "U". Trace this shape, connecting the two smoothly. Repeat this until you have an up-and-down line the length of your border. Put a flower at the top and bottom of each hill and valley. Add leaves, groups of leaves, and more flowers.

Feather Patterns

Many of the feather patterns can be used right from the book. By enlarging or reducing the patterns, they can be made to fit your quilt nicely. You may decide to try your hand at drawing your own feathers on the quilt top. Use the center spines from the patterns and practice the feathers by tracing on paper first. They are really fun, and this exercise will help you machine-quilt them more easily. Once you feel comfortable, mark the spines using the patterns, then draw your own feathers.

Special Circumstances

Some of the patterns need to be copied twice. The second copy will be turned upside down and placed next to the first. The double leaf pattern shown in *Figure 1* is one example.

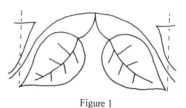

Figure 1

Copy the design. Place the second copy next to the first (*Figure 2*).

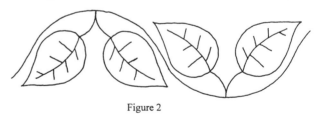

Figure 2

Some patterns show only one-half of the pattern. The other half is the mirror image of the first half. The corner of the large feather border with spray on Plate 33 is an example of this. Trace the pattern onto tracing paper, then turn the paper over. Line up the drawing so that the center matches the center of the right-side-up image. Trace the second half. Sometimes the lines might not match exactly—don't worry, just adjust the lines so that they are smooth.

Other patterns, such as the wreath on Plate 44, show one quarter of the design. Trace the pattern onto tracing paper, then rotate the paper to trace the remaining quarters.

Preparing Your Quilt for Machine Quilting

Marking

We mark our quilt top before it is basted. Choose how you are going to quilt your quilt. Some straight lines may not need to be marked if they follow the piecing of the quilt. However, other straight lines, like diagonals or cross-hatching, may need to be marked. To mark straight lines, we use a quilter's ruler marked with inches, a 45° line, and other necessary measurements.

To use the patterns in this book, simply remove the appropriate page. If you prefer to keep the book intact, you can trace or photocopy the pattern. You may have already done this to adjust the size, as explained earlier. Here are some techniques for transferring the patterns to your quilt top.

Light-colored fabrics: The patterns can simply be traced by placing the pattern under the quilt top.

Dark or print fabrics: Since you cannot easily see through these fabrics to trace the design, there are two ways to put the pattern on your quilt top.

Using a light box: Tape the design to your light box. Place the quilt top on the box and trace.

Making a template: Use lightweight cardboard, template plastic, or Mylar plastic film. Place the template on quilt top and trace the pattern.

Using one of the techniques described above, begin marking your quilt with your preferred marking pencil. When marking designs, it helps to locate the center of the area you are marking on your quilt. Find the center of your design and match the two centers. This helps insure the design is placed evenly on the quilt.

Basting

A well-basted quilt is very important to the success of machine quilting. Please take time to do a good job with this sometimes tedious part of the quiltmaking process. The best way to baste a quilt is to stretch it in a full-sized frame and pin-baste. However, not all of us have the luxury of a full-sized frame. The following is a brief description of the next best way to pin-baste a quilt.

We always cut the backing and batting at least 2" larger than the quilt top. Mark the center of each side of the quilt top and backing. This will allow you to line up your quilt accurately. Lay your quilt backing, wrong side up, either on a large table or on the floor. Using masking tape, tape the sides of the backing to the table or floor. If you are basting to carpeting, use straight pins to secure the backing to the carpet. Lay your batting on the backing, smoothing out any wrinkles. Next, place your pressed and marked quilt top right side up on the batting, matching your center marks so that the top and bottom are lined up. Smooth your quilt top, but do not stretch or distort it. You are ready to pin-baste.

We use size 0 or 1 brass safety pins. For cotton batting, pin every 4", and for polyester batting, pin every 3". Pin from the center out, filling the quilt with the appropriate amount of pins. Leave the pins open until you are completely done pinning the whole top. Remove the tape and close the pins. A new tool called a "Quick Clip" or "Pin Popper" helps with this chore. After the pins are closed, hand baste the outside edge of the quilt top, batting, and backing. This, along with the 2" extra backing, extends your quilt and makes it possible to free-motion quilt your border. You are now ready for machine quilting.

Different Types of Machine Quilting

Straight Line Quilting

Use a walking foot for straight lines, so that the quilt layers feed evenly through the machine. To secure threads for straight stitching, hold the top thread and take one stitch manually (down and up once with the needle). Raise the walking foot and pull the bobbin thread to the top. This allows you to hold the threads as you start sewing and prevents the thread from jamming the machine. Always know where your threads are! Set your stitch-length control for very small stitches; start sewing, then gradually increase the stitch length until you reach the regular stitch length. From where you start stitching to the point you reach the regular stitch length should measure about ¼". There should be at least 8–12 small stitches. The thread ends can now be clipped if you are using nylon thread. If you are using cotton or decorative thread, leave 6" tails, thread onto a needle and bury them in between the layers of the quilt. If you can find "self-threading" needles, it makes this job much easier! The threads may fray if clipped directly off. Save the chore of burying threads to do when you get a fair amount and do them all at once. Continue straight stitching, following your marked line carefully. The walking foot will feed the quilt evenly from the top, matching the feed dogs on the bottom. It is helpful to have a slight fullness in front of the walking foot.

If you are using a regular presser foot, place your hands on either side of the foot and gently help the layers of the quilt feed evenly. Never pull the quilt from in front and behind the presser foot, as this will stretch the row of stitching and distort your quilt.

Stitch length for straight stitching is usually between 10–14 stitches per inch. This is between 2–3 on the stitch length indicator for most machines. Personal preference will determine what works best for you. To end the row of stitching, gradually decrease the stitch length to very small stitches, allowing ¼" as at the beginning of the row to end at the proper place. Clip or bury your threads.

Free-Motion Quilting

Free-motion quilting enables you to do curved designs on the sewing machine. Place the darning foot on the machine and lower the feed dogs. On some machines, the feed dogs cannot be lowered. Instead, a cover is provided to stop the feed-dog motion from feeding the fabric through. To begin, hold the top thread and take one stitch manually (down and up with the needle). Lift up the darning foot and pull the bobbin thread to the top. To secure the stitching, take small stitches, gradually getting larger, for about ¼". Clip threads when you are far enough away to do so, or leave 6" tails, thread them onto a needle and bury them between the quilt layers. Once the feed dogs are lowered (or covered) on your machine, you have no stitch-length control. You control the length of the stitches by moving the quilt. This is like drawing on the quilt with your machine needle. Start very slowly; move your hands and you will make the small stitches needed to secure the threads. When ending the stitching, you also need to take small stitches to secure the threads. Clip or bury threads.

Free-motion quilting is a wonderful technique that takes patience and practice to master. Because you control the stitch length by moving the quilt, it will take time to learn how to maintain a constant stitch size. The faster you move your hands, the larger the stitches; the slower you move your hands, the smaller the stitches.

The speed at which your machine runs also makes a difference in free-motion quilting. Sewing at a very slow speed makes it harder to control your stitching. A medium or medium-high speed seems to work well. The combination of how fast your machine runs and how fast you move your quilt is the formula needed to create a consistent stitch length.

The most important word in free-motion quilting is control. Here are some ideas to help you maintain control while quilting.

• Try not to lift your hands from your work as you sew. Stop sewing with your needle in the down position in your quilt, then reposition your hands. When you lift your hands as you quilt, you lose control and get uneven stitches.

• Think of free-motion quilting as you would think of driving a car—watch the road ahead of you (your design line), not the wheel of the car (the darning foot and needle).

• Use your whole upper body (hands, arms, and shoulders) to control your stitching, not just your fingers.

• Use rubber glove fingers to help control and grip your quilt.

• Remember—practice, practice, practice makes you a better free-motion quilter!

Quilting Your Quilt

Choosing the Order of Machine Quilting
Once your quilt is marked, layered, and basted, it is time to decide the order of machine quilting. We like to start with any straight-line stitching first. This helps stabilize the quilt during the quilting process. Plan to start at the center of the quilt at the top and work from the center to the right. This means that you will only have half or less of the quilt under the arm of the machine. The bulk of the quilt is always moving to the left. When finished on that side, turn the quilt 180° and

start at the top center again and quilt moving to the right. Next, turn the quilt 90° and start at the top center and quilt to the right. And lastly, turn the quilt 180° again and quilt from the top center to the right to complete your straight stitching. Stitch as much of your straight stitching as possible before switching to free-motion quilting. Keep practice samples around and, before your begin the free-motion stitching on your quilt, do a bit of sewing to refresh yourself on the technique (or vice versa, when going from free-motion to straight lines). If there are any problems or tension adjustments necessary, they will happen on your practice samples and not on your quilt. Try to avoid switching between the two types of quilting too often. You will probably need to quilt the inner portion of your quilt first, then the borders. Once you have planned your quilting order, it is time for the next step.

Packaging
Packaging your quilt for machine quilting is very important. In order to have good control of your quilt, whatever its size, you must package properly. Lay your quilt on an area large enough to spread the entire quilt flat. Roll the quilt evenly from each side so that the roll is a few inches away from your quilting line on either side. You may want to use quilter's bicycle clips to hold the rolls closed. For a large quilt, roll tightly, so that it will fit under the arm of the machine. Then roll (or fan-fold back and forth) from the bottom of the quilt to the top, so that it is easy to transport to the sewing area.

Once at your sewing machine, place the quilt in the machine and set the roll against your chest or over your shoulder. For a large quilt, set your ironing board behind you and rest the bulk of the quilt over your shoulder and on the ironing board. Sew the row and continue moving to the right. Repackage as needed to complete the quilt. A large quilt needs to be repackaged often, as it will get out of control easily. For borders, roll the entire quilt from the left and work on one border at a time. Repackage often to keep good control of your quilt. For quilts marked on the diagonal, package from the corners to the middle.

Your Workspace
Do not place your sewing machine table against a wall. The quilt will stop when it hits the wall, making quilting difficult. Always keep the work area clean of items that the quilt might push off the table. Ideally, your sewing machine should be at tabletop height. If your machine sits on a tabletop, use an extension table to bring your work surface away from the machine; if the quilt falls off your machine, it can pull and make it hard to control. If your machine is too high, use a chair that brings you up higher, so your arms are even with the machine.

Problem Solving
• Clean and oil your machine regularly. Machine-quilting is hard on your machine—treat it kindly.

• Dull or damaged sewing machine needles can cause problems. Change your needles periodically.

•Take breaks often, particularly when working on a large quilt. Quilts are heavy and can tire you out. Get up and walk around. When you come back, you will feel refreshed and ready to quilt!

Tension problems:

•If there are bobbin thread loops showing on the top of your quilt, your top tension is too tight. Loosen it by moving your top tension control to a smaller number. If loosening the top tension does not seem to help, you may need to tighten the bobbin tension.

•Some tension problems can be solved by using a straight-stitch throat plate. The layers of the quilt can be pulled down into the opening of a zigzag plate and cause problems with the stitch quality.

•Make sure you are using a good quality thread in your bobbin. Cheap thread can cause tension problems.

•Be kind to yourself! Machine quilters tend to be very critical of themselves as they are quilting. You are doing a great job. When your quilt is finished, stand back and pat yourself on the back for a job well done!

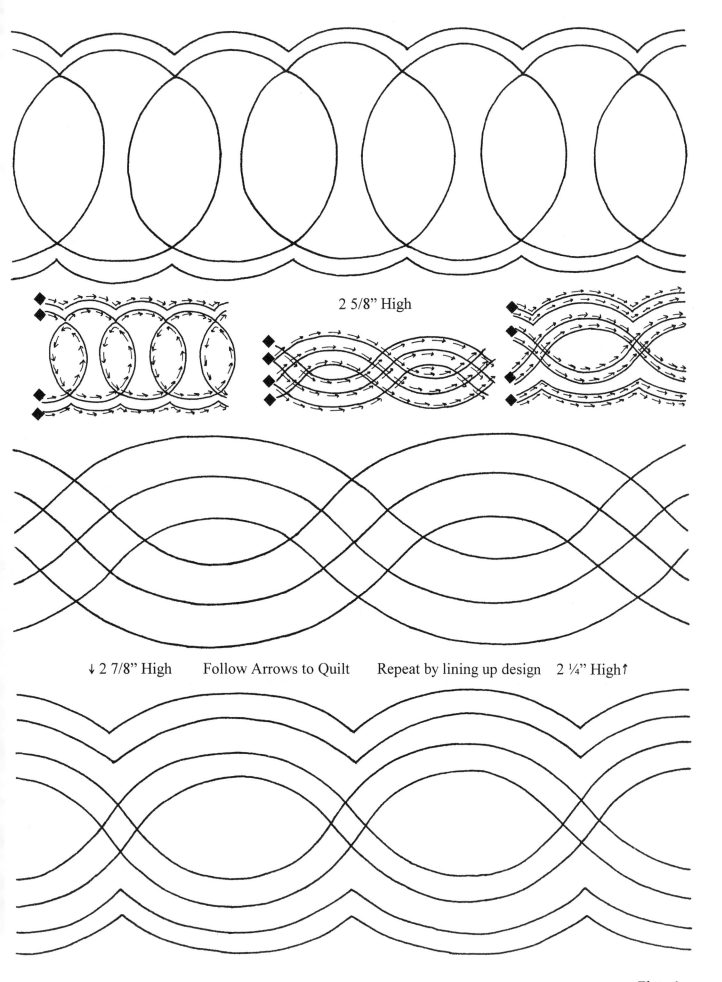

2 5/8" High

↓ 2 7/8" High   Follow Arrows to Quilt   Repeat by lining up design   2 ¼" High↑

Plate 1

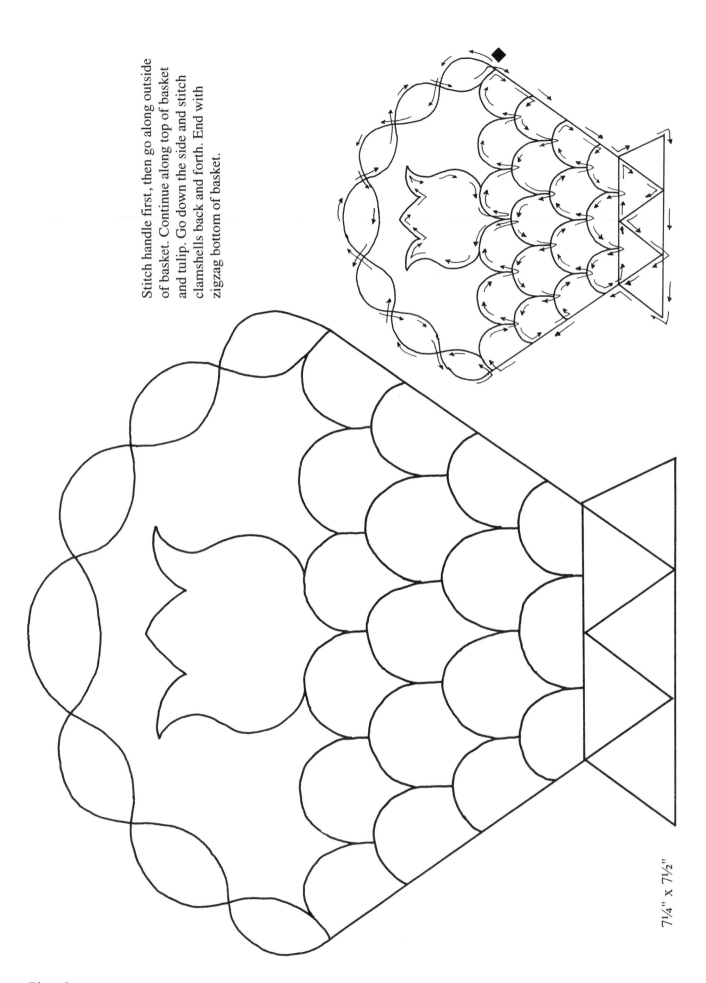

Stitch handle first, then go along outside of basket. Continue along top of basket and tulip. Go down the side and stitch clamshells back and forth. End with zigzag bottom of basket.

7¼" x 7½"

Plate 2

Start at lower right side. Go around 2 loops, then stitch top line of basket handle. Do 2 left loops, then stitch straight line across top of basket. Do inside line of handle, then zigzags, heart, zigzags. Next, go down and up lines of basket. End with base of basket.

7" x 9½"

Plate 3

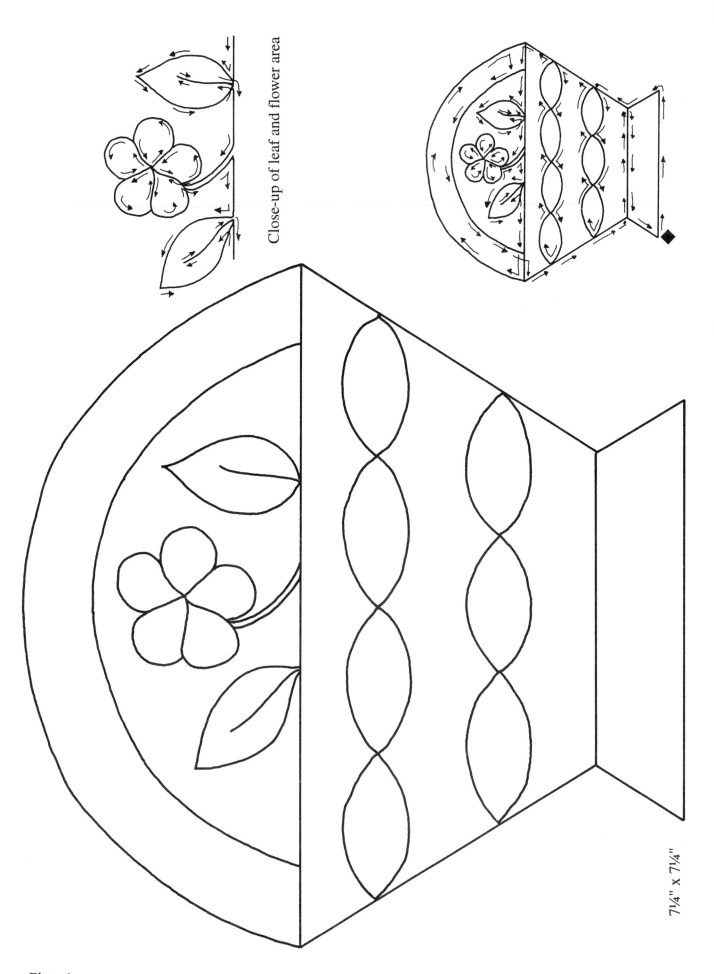

Close-up of leaf and flower area

7¼" x 7¼"

Plate 4

Close-up of tulip stitching order

9" diagonally
7¼" straight across

Plate 5

Start in center. Do the outside and inside of corner shape, then only the outer line of smaller shape. Continue all around. From the center circle, go back and stitch inner line of the four middle shapes.

7¼" square

Plate 6

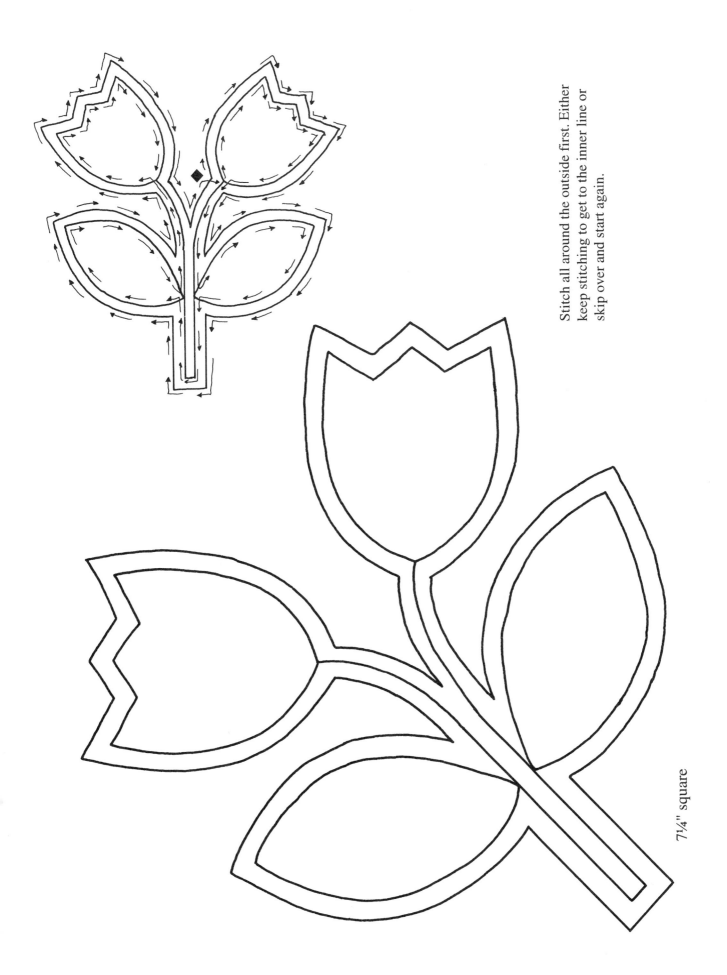

Stitch all around the outside first. Either keep stitching to get to the inner line or skip over and start again.

7¼" square

Plate 7

Close-up of flower stitching order

7¼" square

Plate 8

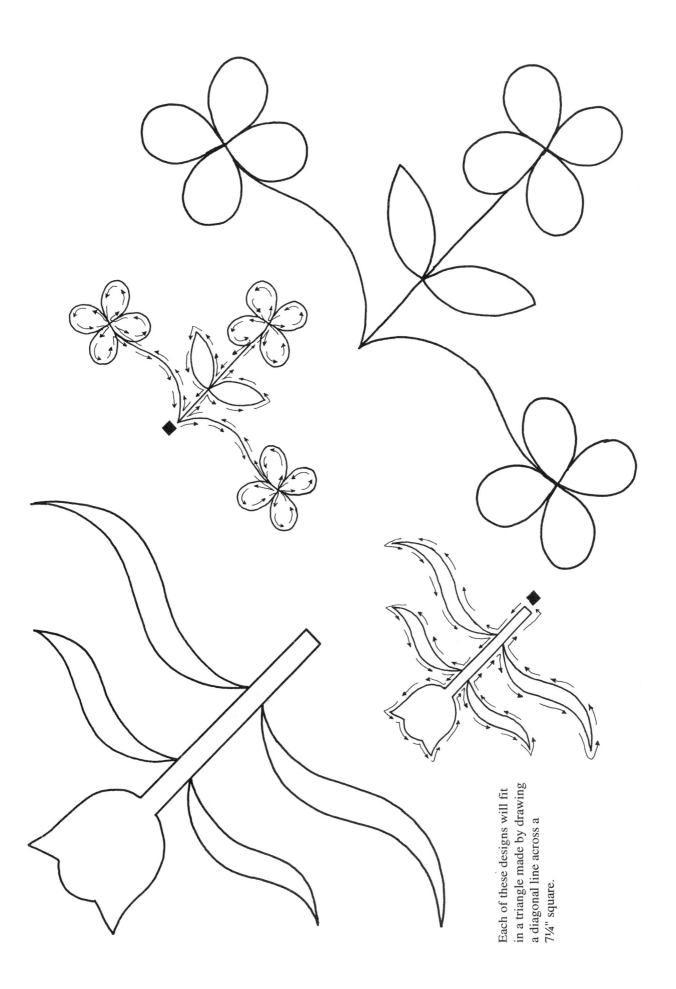

Each of these designs will fit in a triangle made by drawing a diagonal line across a 7¼" square.

Plate 9

Start in center. Stitch leaves and bud. Do tulip next. Continue around second bud and tulip.

7¼" square

Plate 10

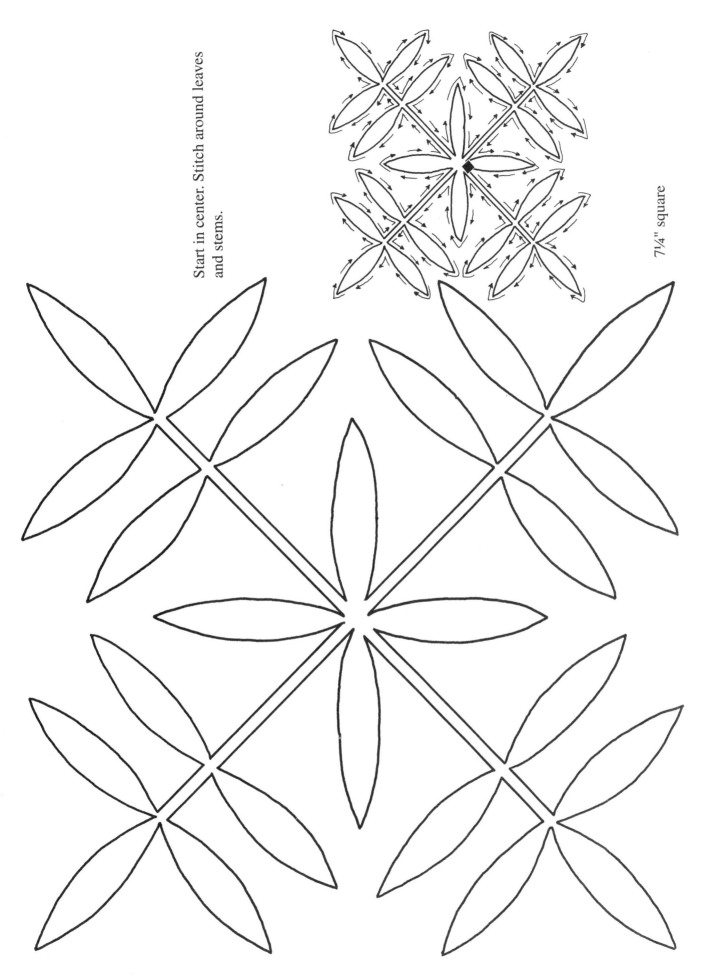

Start in center. Stitch around leaves and stems.

7¼" square

Plate 11

4" x 8"

4¼" square

Draw leaf in desired arrangement.
Add vine to connect leaves.

Leaf pair can be placed in many ways -
all the same direction, alternate one up
and one down, etc.

Plate 12

Start with the center lines and diamond shapes. Go up and around each "arm". Start again at the outside line, stitch around. Travel to the inner line of star and stitch around.

7" tip to tip (diagonally)
7½" straight across

Plate 13

It will take four passes of stitches to complete the design.

Each repeat will be started again.

2½" x 8" repeat

3½" x 9¼" repeat

Plate 14

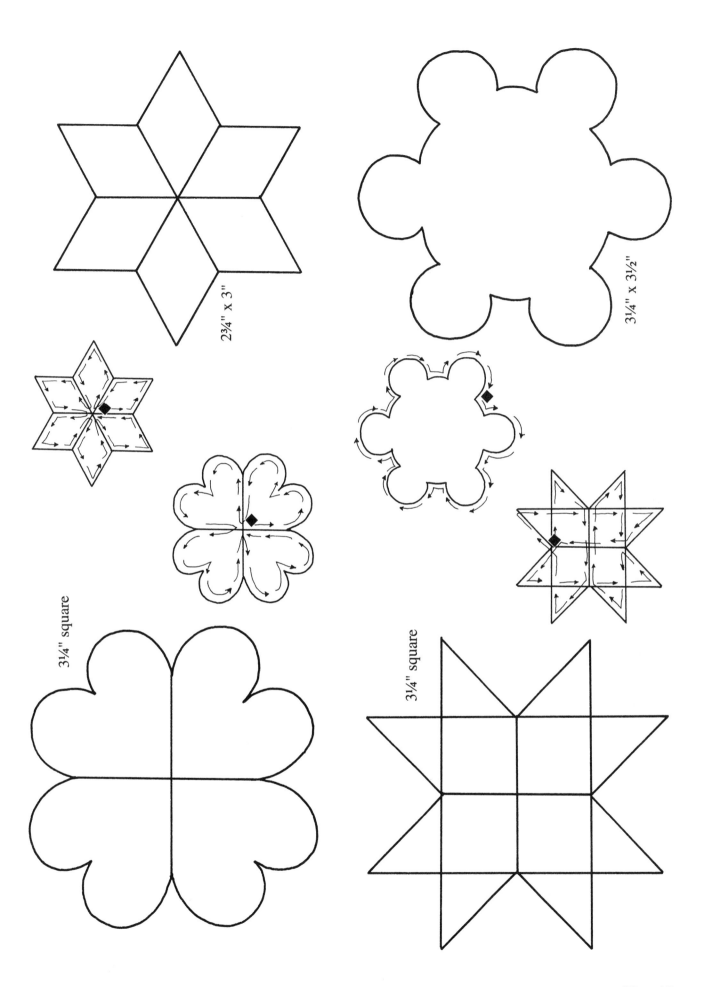

2¾" x 3"

3¼" x 3½"

3¼" square

3¼" square

Plate 15

Reverse design as shown in small drawing.

Each repeat will be started again.

3¼" x 9¼" repeat

3¾" x 7" repeat

Plate 16

6 ¾" High, 6 ½" Repeat

Start sewing at ◆. Follow first cable arc to the right, turn, tracing short
amount of next cable, turn and follow second cable arc to the left, turn,
tracing short amount of cable down, turn and follow third cable arc to
the right, turn, tracing short amount of cable down, turn and follow
forth cable arc to the left, ending stitching here. Repeat steps to complete
cable border.

Plate 17

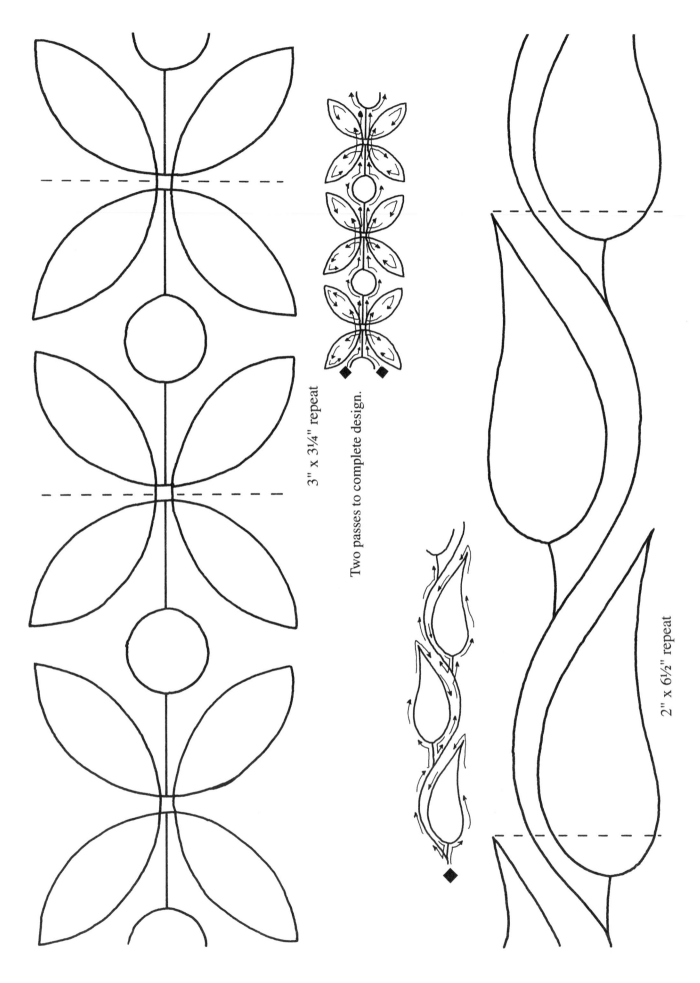

3" x 3¼" repeat

Two passes to complete design.

2" x 6½" repeat

Plate 18

Flower - go around outer petals, then stitch lines around center. Come out to continue along stem.

3" x 6½" repeat

3¼" x 6¼" repeat

Plate 19

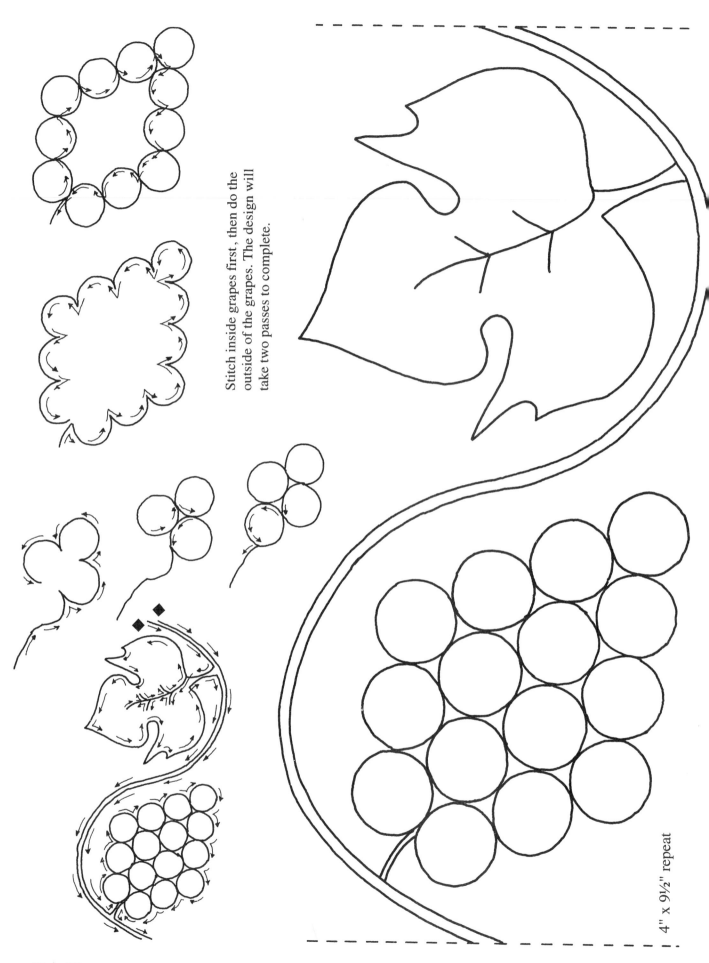

Stitch inside grapes first, then do the outside of the grapes. The design will take two passes to complete.

4" x 9½" repeat

Plate 20

6" x 9"

Plate 21

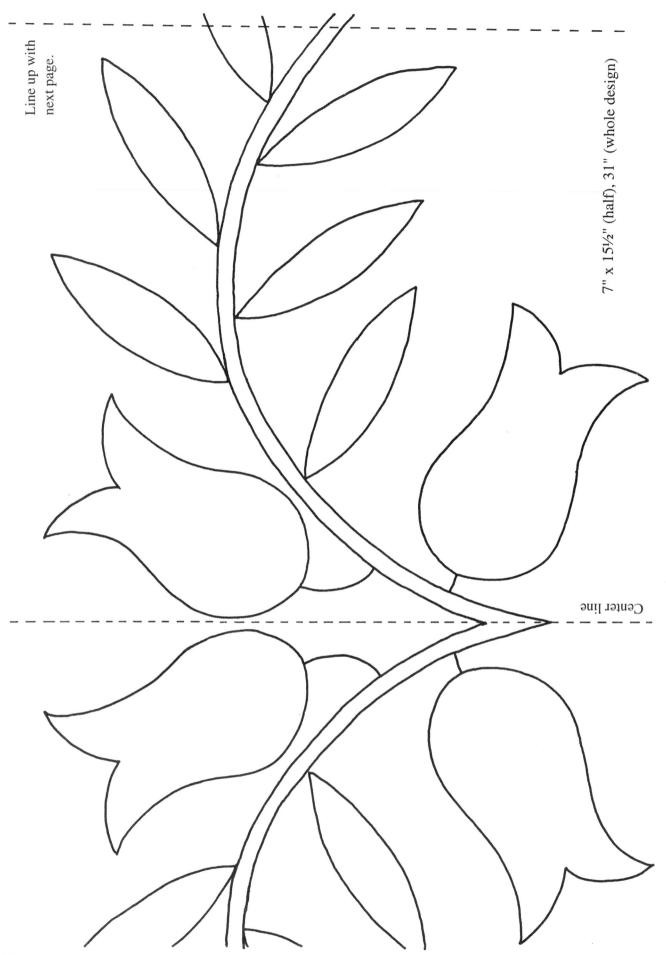

Line up with next page.

7" x 15½" (half), 31" (whole design)

Center line

Plate 22

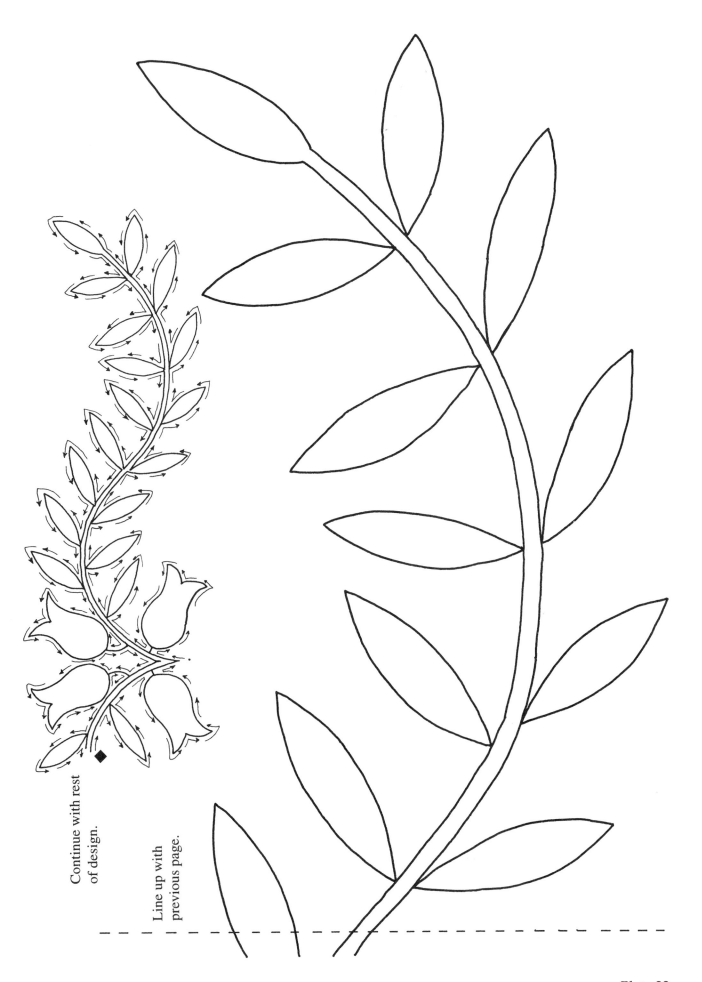

Continue with rest of design.

Line up with previous page.

Plate 23

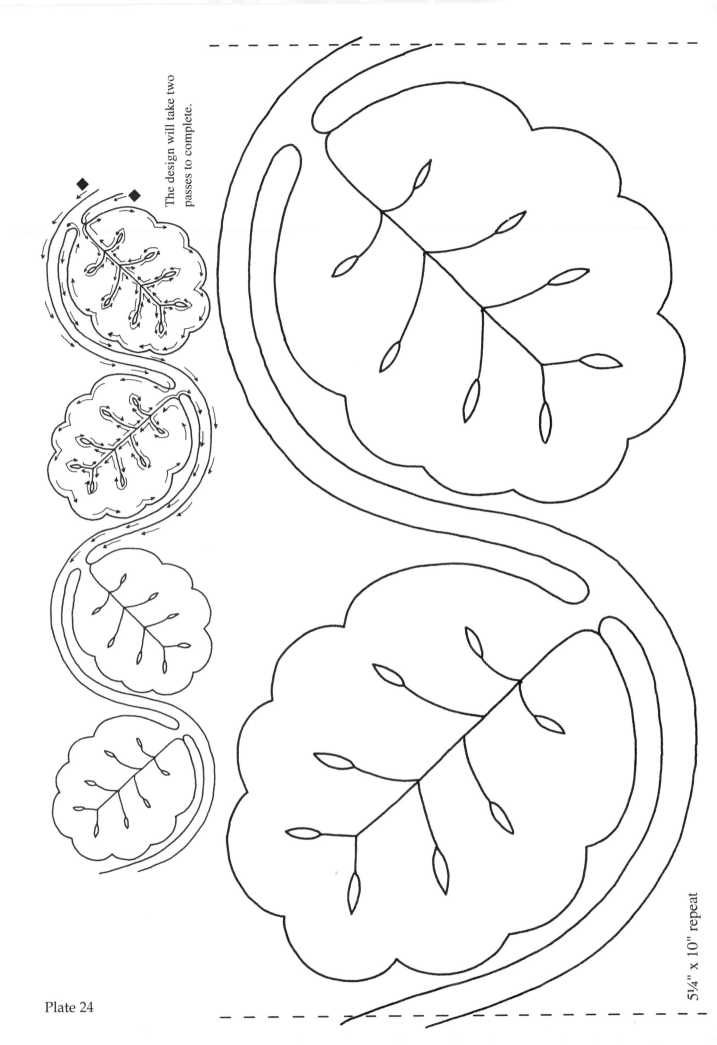

The design will take two passes to complete.

5¼" x 10" repeat

Plate 24

Each motif will be stitched separately.

6¼" x 9¾"

Plate 25

Instructions for using these elements is included in the "How To" section.

Plate 26

Plate 27

5 7/8" High, 8 ¾" Repeat
Quilt following arrows as shown for first four rows.
Repeat for second four rows.

Plate 28

Cable Corner
Fit into cable design at cross-hatching.

Plate 29

Feather Sewing Directions

Sew center line (spine) first. Some feather designs have no center line so start with the feathers.

Go back to the start. Begin stitching first feather at the center spine line. Sew around the feather and down along the top part of the next feather.

Stitch the second feather by sewing as close as possible back up along the line you have already sewn. Complete the feather by sewing along the top part of the next feather until you reach the spine.

Repeat until all the feathers on one side of the center spine are sewn.

Return to starting point and start sewing feathers on the other side of the center spine.

Continue stitching feathers until the second side is complete.

The drawing shows a double line of quilting stitches between feathers. Your quilting should be as close as possible to the same line and ideally could be one single line. The double row is exaggerated to help show how to stitch.

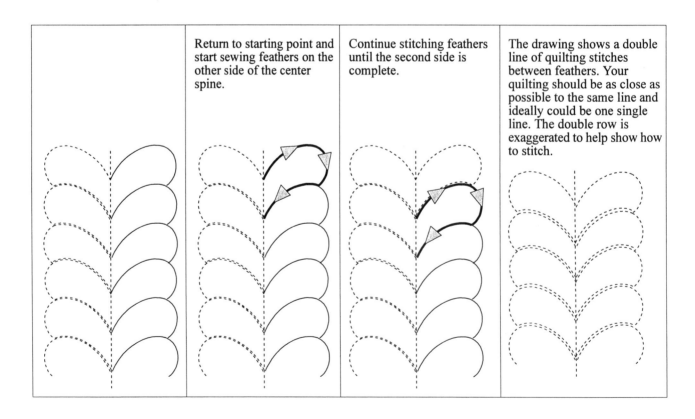

Plate 30

Large Feather Border with Spray   Feather Quilting- See Feather Sewing Directions
7 ¾" High
For complete border design, line up three pages of patterns along dotted lines.

Plate 31

Plate 32

Layout for Large Feather Border with Spray

Large Feather Border with Spray Corner
7 ¾" High

Plate 33

Feather Quilting- See Feather Sewing Directions

6 ¼" High, 9 ¾" Long

Plate 34

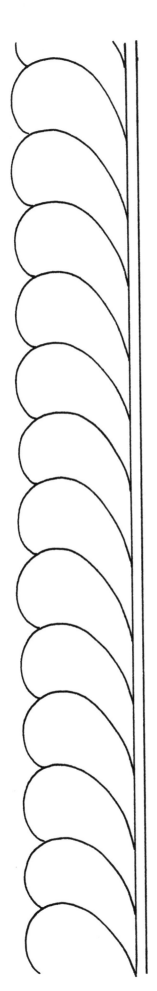

1 3/8" High   Feather Quilting- See Feather Sewing Directions

3" High, 7" Repeat   Feather Quilting- See Feather Sewing Directions

Plate 35

2 ¼" High, 7 ¼" Long
Follow Arrows for Quilting

Layout for Sashing or Border

5 ½" Square   Feather Quilting- See Feather Sewing Directions

Plate 36

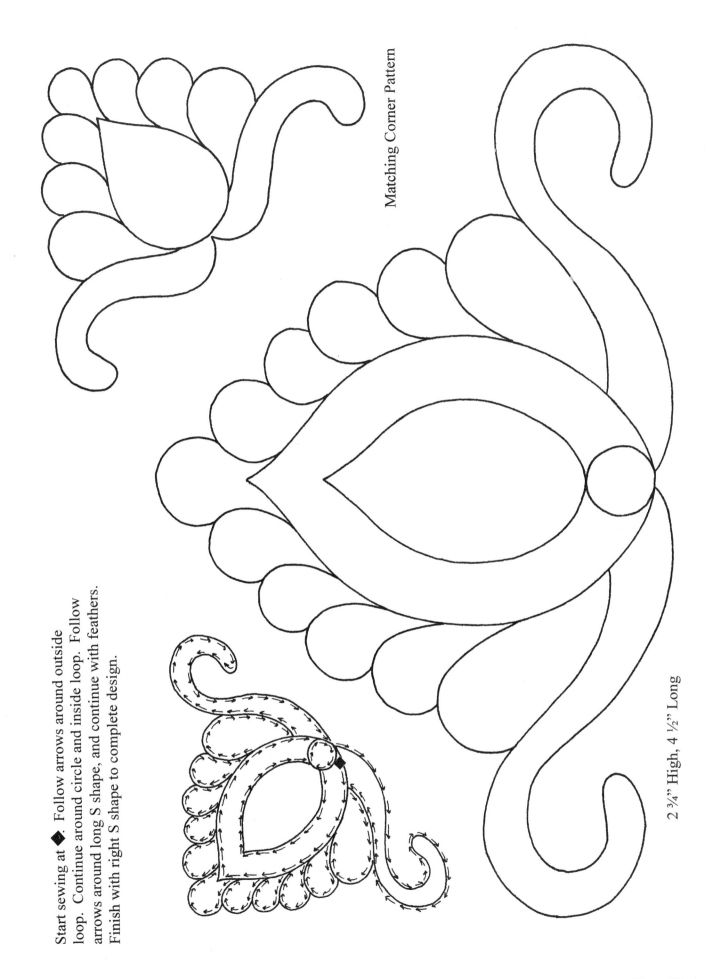

Matching Corner Pattern

Start sewing at ◆. Follow arrows around outside loop. Continue around circle and inside loop. Follow arrows around long S shape, and continue with feathers. Finish with right S shape to complete design.

2 ¾" High, 4 ½" Long

Plate 37

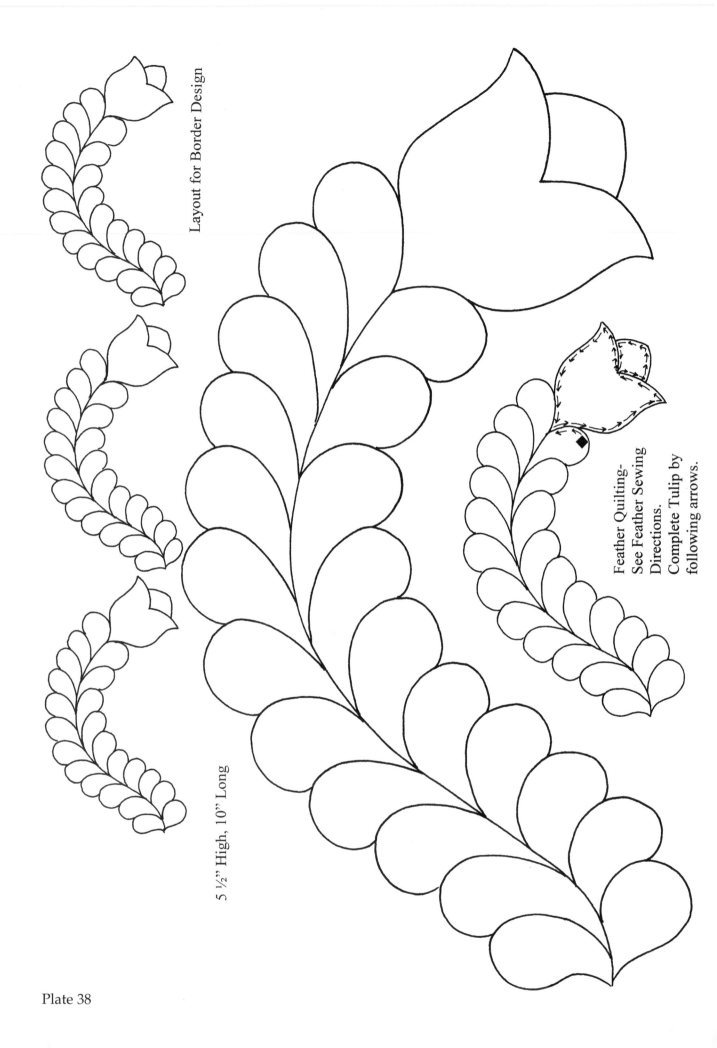

Layout for Border Design

5 ½" High, 10" Long

Feather Quilting-
See Feather Sewing
Directions.
Complete Tulip by
following arrows.

Plate 38

Feather Quilting- See Feather Sewing Directions

Cross-hatching- Free motion back and forth retracing on feathers, as shown. Repeat for opposite direction.

6 ¼" High, 7 1/8" Long

Plate 39

7 1/8" High, 6" Repeat

Feather Quilting- See Feather Sewing Directions

Plate 40

6" High, 6" Repeat

Quilt Feathers First- See Feather Sewing Directions

Cable Directions- Start sewing at ◆. Follow arrows carefully, tracing along feathers, continuing back and forth along cable arcs. Repeat for all cables.

Plate 41

Large Feather Wreath- 14"
Medium Feather Wreath- 9 ¾"

One-quarter of design
Line up along dotted lines

Feather Quilting- See Feather Sewing Directions

Plate 42

Center Star- Start at smallest star. Free-motion quilt following arrows. Make securing stitches. Lift presser foot and move to next star. Make securing stitches and free-motion quilt around the star. Repeat until all stars are done. Clip threads.

Center Star- 4 ½" tip to tip

Feather or Star for
Center of Feather Wreath

Small Feather Wreath- 5 ¼"

Plate 43

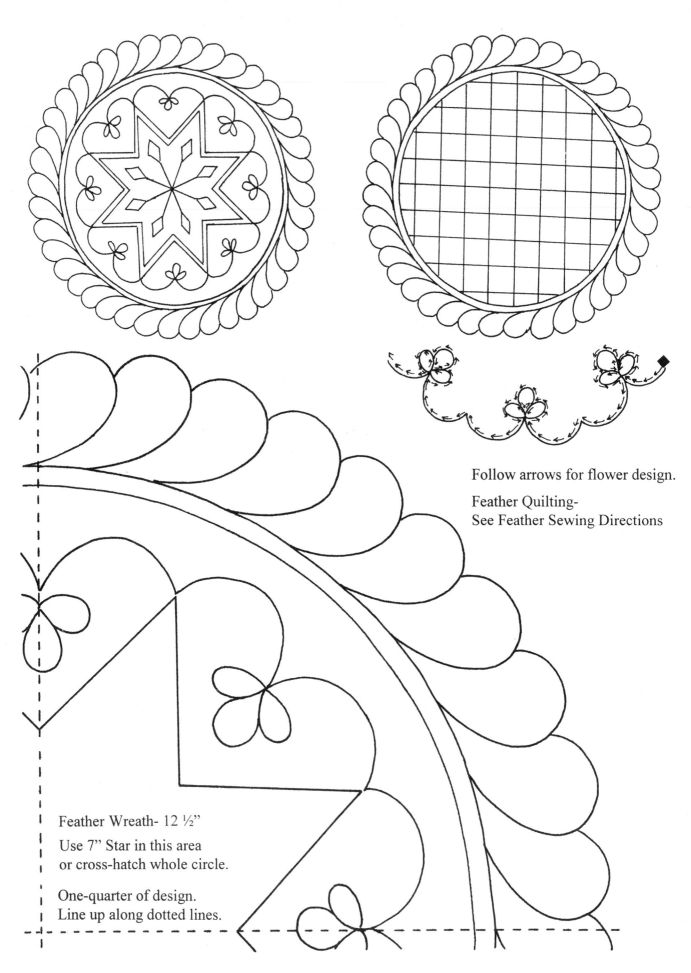

Follow arrows for flower design.

Feather Quilting-
See Feather Sewing Directions

Feather Wreath- 12 ½"

Use 7" Star in this area
or cross-hatch whole circle.

One-quarter of design.
Line up along dotted lines.

Plate 44